9.30

MW01041953

The Life Cycle of a
BEE

Jill Bailey

Illustrated by
Jackie Harland

Reading Consultant:
Diana Bentley

Life Cycles

Editor: Janet De Saulles

First published in 1989 by
Wayland (Publishers) Limited
61 Western Road, Hove
East Sussex, BN3 1JD, England

© Copyright 1989 Wayland (Publishers) Limited

British Library Cataloguing in Publication Data
Bailey, Jill
  The life cycle of a bee.
  1. Bees
  I. Title.   II. Harland, Jackie   III. Series
  595.79'9

  ISBN 1–85210–621–2

Typeset in the UK by DP Press Limited, Sevenoaks, Kent
Printed and bound by Casterman S.A., Belgium

Notes for parents and teachers
Each title in this series has been specially written and
designed as a first natural history book for young readers.
For less able readers there are introductory captions,
while the more detailed text explains each illustration.

Contents

All the words that are
in **bold** are explained in
the glossary on page 31.

A bee is an **insect.**

In this picture, you can see how the bee's body is made up of three parts – a head, a **thorax** and a long **abdomen**. On the head are two large eyes, a pair of feelers for touching and smelling, and a mouth. There are three pairs of legs and two pairs of stiff, see-through wings joined to the bee's thorax. The abdomen contains the stomach. At the tip of the abdomen is a sting.

The bee feeds on **nectar** and **pollen** from flowers.

The bee sucks up the nectar with its long tongue and stores it in its stomach. Pollen sticks to its furry body. The bee scrapes it off with special combs on its legs, and stores it in pollen baskets made of stiff hairs on its back legs. Then the worker bee takes the nectar and pollen back to the nest for the other bees to share.

Lots of bees live together in a nest.

Wild honeybees build their nests in hollow trees or caves. Each nest is made up of several large flat **combs** made of wax. Each comb contains lots of tiny six-sided cells. Some cells contain the bees' eggs and their young. Others contain food stores of honey and pollen. Tame bees, that belong to beekeepers, build their honeycombs in special wooden **hives**.

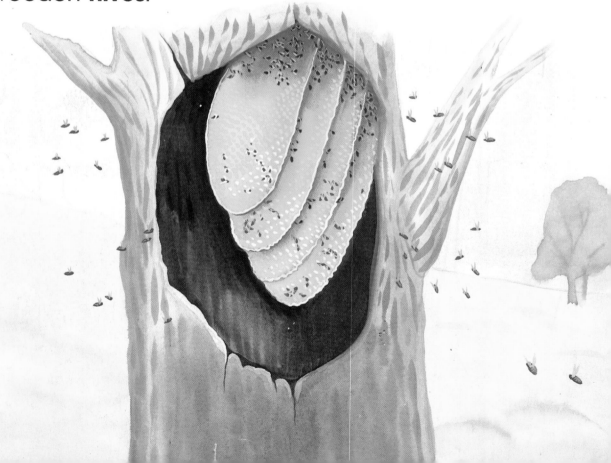

queen bee

worker bee

The **queen bee** rules the nest.

Many thousands of honeybees may live in one nest. The queen bee is the mother of them all. She is larger than the other bees. The worker bees are all females. During the summer, there are also some male bees in the nest. They are called drones. The drones are bigger than the workers.

drone

The queen bee lays her eggs.

The queen bee spends her whole life laying eggs. The worker bees feed and clean her. She lays each egg in its own wax cell on the comb. Some cells near the edge of the comb are larger than the others. Here, the queen lays special eggs that will **hatch** into drones.

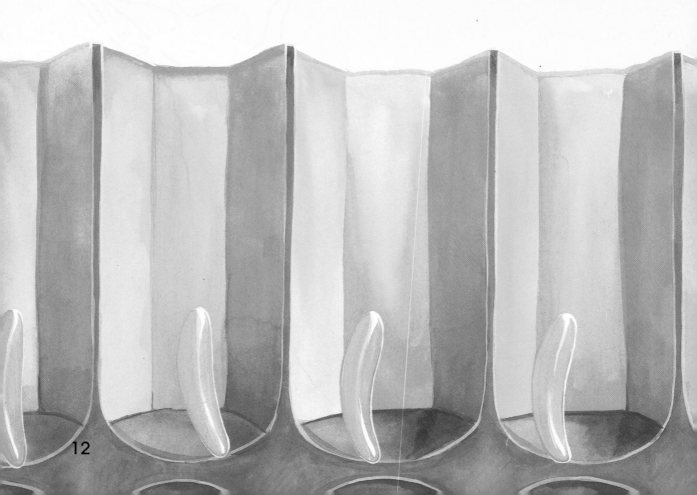

13

After three days each egg becomes a tiny **grub**.

The grub of the bee is called a **larva**. It is blind and helpless. The worker bees feed it by dribbling food from their mouths. At first the larva gets a special food made inside the worker bees. Later, it is fed on honey and pollen. Drone larvae get more food than worker larvae.

The larva changes into a **pupa**.

Five days after hatching, the larva stops feeding. The worker bees cover the cell with a wax lid to keep the larva safe. The larva is now called a pupa. It takes about eight days for the pupa to change into a bee.

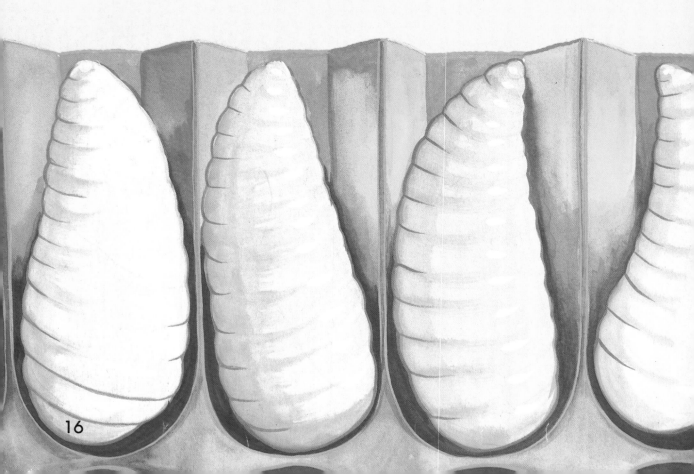

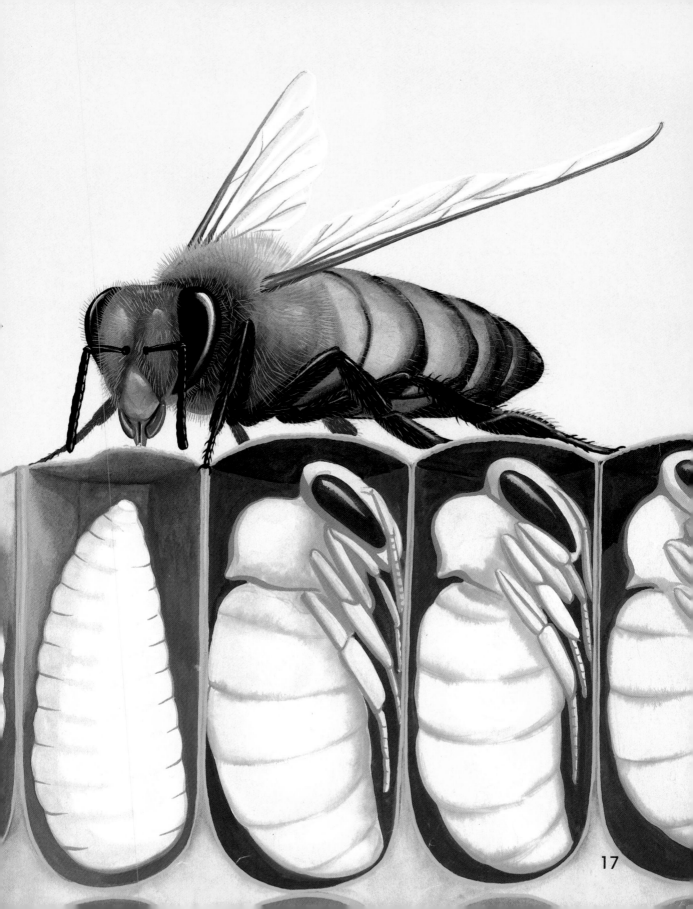

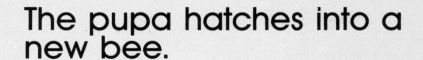

The pupa hatches into a new bee.

The new bee chews its way through the lid of the cell. The workers come to help it. Immediately, it is put to work, cleaning cells for new eggs. Soon, it will help to feed the grubs. After about two weeks, the young bee can produce wax from its abdomen and it helps to build and repair the comb.

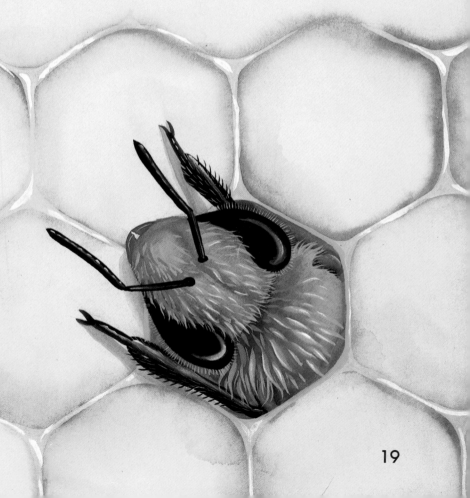

The bees bring food to the nest.

Older bees collect nectar and pollen. They give some of the nectar to the bees back at the nest. To make honey, the bees chew the nectar and mix it with a special liquid from their mouths. Then they put it in a cell to set. When the honey is ripe, the bees seal it in the cell with wax. The pollen is also stored in cells.

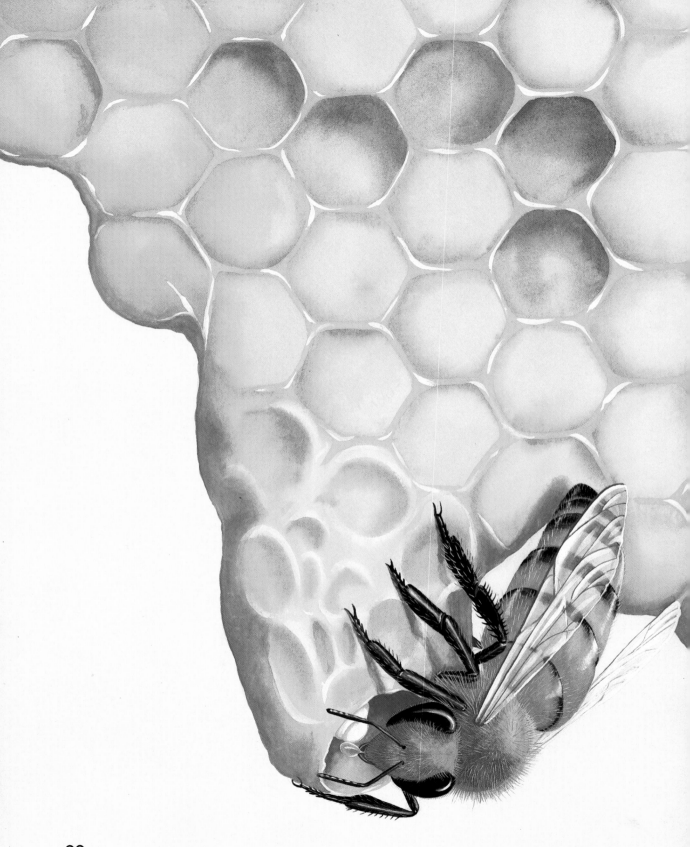

The bees feed the new queen grubs.

If the old queen dies, or if the nest gets too crowded, the workers prepare special new queen cells near the edge of the comb. The grubs which hatch in these cells are fed on a special food called **royal jelly**. These grubs will become new queen bees.

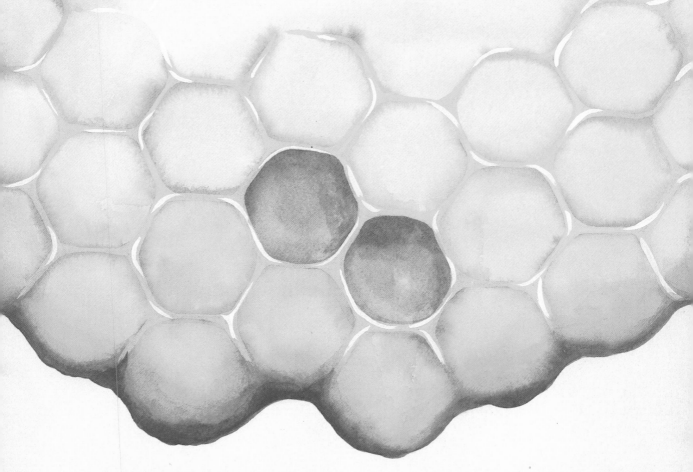

The bees swarm.

If the nest is overcrowded the old queen leaves before the new queens hatch. She leaves surrounded by thousands of the workers. This huge crowd of bees is called a swarm. The swarm settles in a tree while scout bees look for a good place to make a new nest. Then the swarm flies to the new home, and the old queen starts laying eggs again.

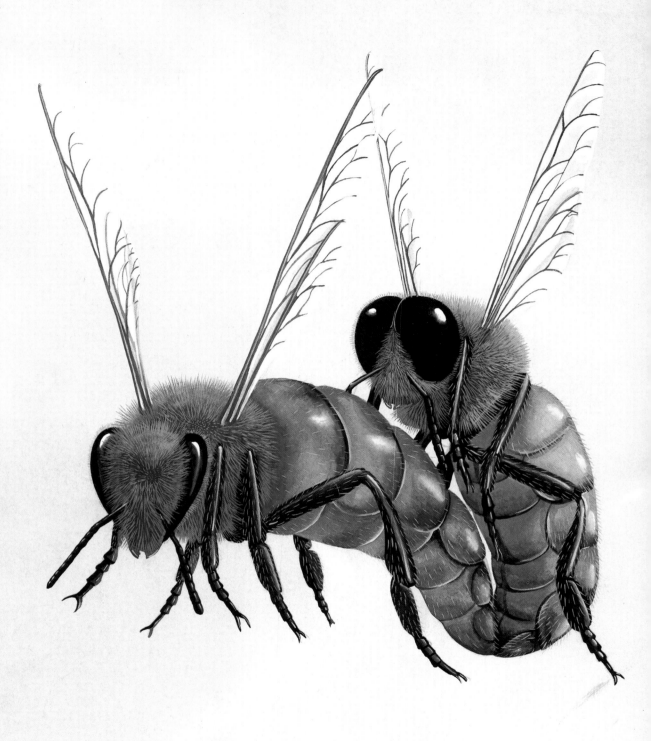

The young queen and the drones fly off to **mate**.

When the first new queen hatches, she kills the other young queens with her sting. Then the new queen flies off with all the drones on her marriage flight. She mates with several of the drones, then returns to the nest and starts laying eggs to produce new worker bees. The drones soon die, or are driven away by the workers.

Looking at bees.

Bees have nasty stings, so it is not safe to touch them. You can have a lot of fun, though, looking at bees in your garden or local park. There are many different kinds of bees. Lawn bees are red and furry and live in grass. Bumblebees are much bigger than honeybees, and live in nests in the ground. Some bumblebees are yellow and grey, others are red and black. Leafcutter bees cut off pieces of leaf and roll them up to make their cells. How many different bees can you spot?

Lawn bee

Bumblebees

Leafcutter bee

The life cycle of a bee.

How many stages of the life cycle can you remember? Here is the life cycle of a queen bee.

Glossary

Abdomen The rear part of an insect's body. It contains the stomach and the eggs.

Combs Flat sheets of wax covered with six-sided cells in a bee's nest.

Grub The larva of an insect.

Hatch To break out of an egg.

Hives Bees which are kept by beekeepers live in hives.

Insect A small animal with six legs and one or two pairs of wings. Its body is divided into three parts.

Larva A baby insect that does not look like its parents. When there are more than one, they are called larvae.

Mate This is when male (father) and female (mother) animals join together. This is how a baby animal is made.

Nectar A sugary liquid found in flowers.

Pollen The yellow powder produced by flowers.

Pupa The resting stage when a larva changes into an adult insect.

Queen bee The female bee which lays the eggs.

Royal jelly A special food produced by worker bees. It is fed to the larvae that will become queen bees.

Thorax The middle part of an insect's body. It bears the legs and the wings.

Finding out more

Here are some books to read to find out more about bees.

Animal Homes by Malcolm Penny (Wayland, 1987)
Insects by Anthony Wootton (Usborne, 1979)
Nature Study – Bees and Wasps by Anne Smith
    (Wayland, 1989)
The Insect World by Keith Porter (Macmillan, 1986)

Index

Date Due

FEB 14			OCT 3 2
nk			OCT 2 3